DO
NOTHING
CHRISTMAS
IS COMING

AN ADVENT
CALENDAR WITH
A DIFFERENCE

STEPHEN COTTRELL

DO
NOTHING
CHRISTMAS
IS COMING

AN ADVENT
CALENDAR WITH
A DIFFERENCE

STEPHEN COTTRELL

CHURCH HOUSE
PUBLISHING

Church House Publishing
Church House
Great Smith Street
London SW1P 3AZ

ISBN 978 0 7151 4212 7

Published 2008 by Church House Publishing
Copyright © Stephen Cottrell 2008

Second impression 2009

The opinions expressed in this book are those of the author
and do not necessarily reflect the official policy of the General
Synod or The Archbishops' Council of the Church of England.

Printed in England by The Cromwell Press Group, Trowbridge, Wilts

For my family with whom I have shared so many
Happy Christmases

With thanks to Kathryn Pritchard and all at Church
House Publishing for their support with this little book

What is the point of a once-a-year celebration of consumption and excess in a society entirely dedicated to those broad-buttocked deities month in, month out? Each Christmas we eat too much, drink too much and buy too much. So just what makes December different?

Andrew Marr

A lovely thing about Christmas is that it's compulsory, like a thunderstorm, and we all go through it together.

Garrison Keillor

Contents

Introduction

People who know about computers tell me that they need to be defragged on a regular basis. I don't really know what 'defragged' means – I am to computer technology what King Herod was to child-minding – but it is something to do with reversing the fragmentation that takes place when computers store different bits of a document in different places on the hard drive. Every time the file is accessed the computer has to search the hard drive to gather all the pieces together. This causes computers to slow down and crash. It's a bit like cutting up a written document and storing different bits of it in different folders in different drawers in the filing cabinet, and then having to search through the whole thing to piece it back together every time you want to retrieve the document.

Defragging the computer prevents this problem by rearranging the broken up parts of a file and putting them close together on the hard drive, thus increasing speed and performance. Once you've finished defragging you can reboot and start afresh.

What's all this got to do with Christmas, I hear you say? Well, life needs defragmenting. Life needs rebooting. And Christmas is the time when you are most likely to notice the problem. There are so many different programmes running at once. So many plates spinning. The different bits of our life pull in different and conflicting directions. We are running up the down escalator of the 24/7 culture and can't help feeling that there must be another way.

And before I get completely tangled in this web of muddled metaphors, let me put it plainly: *I* am in danger of crashing. *I* am fragmented. *I* haven't got life worked out, and I certainly haven't got Christmas worked out. It is one of the most joyful times of year. It is also one of the most stressful. It is laden with expectations. It is often overtaken with grief. It can easily be the time of year when all the conflicting demands and expectations that we experience every day in our dispersed and fragmented lives seem at their worse. It might be the season of good will, but it feels like the last straw on an already overburdened camel. Wise men would not ride this one.

There must be an up escalator – another way of inhabiting the world where the fragments of our lives are gathered together and we can live in a more holistic way. There must be another way of celebrating Christmas, where its joys and promises can help put life back together again. So this book offers you a conversation between the imagined voice of the sort of frazzled and fragmented person that many of us become at Christmas, and my own reflections and suggestions on how to make sense of this and start sorting things out. If you need your Christmas (and your life) defragged and rebooted, read on.

1   December

"Groan. It's the first day of December. I've got about a hundred Christmas cards to write (and several ghastly round robin letters to read). The kids are opening their chocolate Advent calendars and I've just got this poxy book. What is this all about?"

The four stages of Christmas are:

1.   You believe in Father Christmas.

2.   You don't believe in Father Christmas.

3.   You are Father Christmas.

4.   You look like Father Christmas.

I think I'm between stages three and four. I give a lot of presents. I'm getting older. I remember the magic of believing in Father Christmas – of waking up on Christmas morning with presents at the foot of my bed. I remember the sober realities of not believing, of horizons narrowing to what is before me.

And now with Christmas just around the corner (and all those cards still to write), I'm surrounded by escalating busyness and can feel my stress level starting to rise. 'Is there something else to believe in?' is the question so many people are asking. I think the answer is yes, but there is lots of sorting out to do along the way.

- Write a Christmas wish list – not things you want to consume or purchase, but things to believe in, things to hope for.

- Prune your Christmas card list.

- At least make sure it is charity cards you buy.

- Don't write 'Must see you this year' on your cards unless you actually mean it. And if you don't mean it, why are you sending this card at all?

- Help save the planet and send an email-card, and then a note about which charity the money saved has been sent to.

- And with all the time you've saved, put your feet up for an hour!

Why is Christmas like a day at the office? You do all the work and the fat guy with the suit gets all the credit.

Ogden Nash

2 December

"Twenty-three shopping days to go. And all the family coming to stay. And all expecting a present. Where am I going to find the time, let alone the money!"

It has been said that Christmas begins sometime around the first of December with an office party and ends when you finally realize what you spent – on 5 April the next year. It is certainly the great consumer festival. Cash tills bleep and hum in a feeding frenzy of spending, and shops that are usually lean and quiet spring into action hoping that a fat December will keep them going for the rest of the year.

Giving and receiving presents is a wonderful part of the Christmas tradition. It can also be a monstrous burden. We spend money we can't afford on presents nobody really wants. Sometimes I find myself looking at the great orgy of present opening that greets Christmas morning, the huge expectations and the inevitable disappointments, and it feels a million miles away from whatever it is that Christmas was supposed to be about. I switch on the television and I am bombarded by adverts telling me what I need and what I want and the glamorous lifestyle they deliver. Is there another way of thinking about presents?

- Give everyone the same thing. Choose one book that you love and buy everyone a copy.

- Instead of spending a fortune at the shops – let alone the time and hassle – make everyone a jar of marmalade, or pickle some onions. This could all be done in one evening.

- Agree with your family and friends that you will all buy and receive *one* present with an agreed price limit.

- Buy everyone a present from charities such as Christian Aid or Oxfam and help the world in the process. Contact www.oxfam.org.uk or www.christianaid.org.uk. And there are lots of other charities that offer ways of giving presents that help others.

Please note: Christmas has been cancelled this year. Apparently you told Santa you have been good this year. He died laughing.

Anonymous

3 December

"So tell me what you want, what you really, really want . . ."

There is a great story about a government minister who was asked this question by a newspaper who were running an article on what famous people wanted for Christmas. Not wanting to appear too grasping, he said that he rather liked those bottles of stem ginger that you see in the shops around this time of year. And so the article ran: 'We asked leading figures what they wanted for Christmas. The Archbishop of Canterbury said he wanted an end to the violence in Iraq. The Dali Lama said he wanted peace in the Middle East. The Pope said he wanted an end to poverty. The Minister for Trade and Industry said he wanted a jar of stem ginger.'

When people ask me what I want, I am never quite sure what to say. It already seems that I have far too much stuff, and don't really want more of it. Then people retort by saying, 'Oh it must be nice to be you, having everything!' But what is it that I really want? And how do I find out?

- Dare to find some time to stop and be still, if only for a few minutes. Ask what truly brings you joy and comfort, and see how this could become part of your Christmas celebration.

- In which case, for Christmas I would like a long walk in the countryside . . . or a hot bath . . . or to lie on the floor and listen to a piece of music. But what about you? What is your deepest wish? What would you *really* like?

- And what do you want for the world?

Blessed is the season which engages the whole world in a conspiracy of love.

Hamilton Wright Mabie

4 December

"Why is it always snowing on the adverts? Can anyone actually remember the last time it snowed at Christmas? If I see another perfect little family sitting round their perfect little Christmas tree, beaming with yuletide joy as they pull crackers and open presents, I swear I will take an axe to the television set!"

People often accuse the church of peddling myths at Christmas. Well, the real Christmas myth has to be the one you see on the TV commercials night after night, presenting this happy picture of doting parents and satisfied children enjoying a stress-free celebration.

The story of family life that is at the heart of the Christmas story is radically different. Mary is a teenage mum. Pregnant outside of marriage, she is almost abandoned and then wonderfully supported by her husband-to-be. About to give birth, they travel great distances in order to conform to the tax regulations of an occupying foreign power. There is nowhere for the child to be born, so Mary ends up giving birth in a cowshed at the back of a pub. There was no midwife. No gas and air. No clean sheets. No epidural.

The Christmas story we find in the Bible is much closer to real family life than the commercials: real people struggling with enormous challenges, supporting each other through enormous difficulties. What can I do to show my family – with all their idiosyncrasies, frustrations, challenges and delights – that I love and support them?

- Pick up the phone . . .

- . . . or at least send a text or an email, but not one that adds to people's burdens, demanding a reply – just something to let someone know that you are thinking of them.

- Imagine yourself into the shoes of a family member, especially one you're finding difficult. What are you like to them? And what are the challenges they are facing?

- Try to spend a few moments each day thinking and praying for your family. Christmas is often the time when families get together and often the time when they fall apart. Think through what your family is facing, and pour some goodwill into them.

If only God would give me some clear sign. Like making a large deposit in my name in a Swiss bank.

Woody Allen

5 December

"The credit card bill for last month arrived this morning. And, no, I haven't started my Christmas shopping yet. Need I say more?"

Buying things on credit is like drinking too much. There is the initial heady excitement, but there is a long hangover to follow. Never in the field of human commerce has so much been owed by so many to so few. It's so easy, so beguiling, so seductive – to see what we think we want, to offer that little oblong of plastic, to tap in our PIN, to receive the fleeting gratification of the purchase, a temporary high, the need for another fix, another purchase. We call it retail therapy. Retail addiction would be more accurate.

Odd, when the Christmas story is about God coming to earth to pay our debts, to show us how to live, to show us what being human could look like, that we should respond by running up more debt.

- Cut up the credit card now. If things are really bad, then there's really no alternative.

- Only use cash; it will help you keep a better check on how much you are spending.

- Do another quick bit of mental arithmetic. How much do you earn? How much can you afford? What can you realistically spend on Christmas this year?

- For help with debt, phone the National Debtline on 0808 8084000 or go to the Citizens Advice Bureau website, www.adviceguide.org.uk. The Christian stewardship website www.stewardship.org.uk also has lots of helpful information including a Christmas challenge and top ten tips for financial management at Christmas. Or look at the Church of England's Matter of Life and Debt pages at www.cofe.anglican.org/debt.

- And what other debts do you have? What outstanding claims of love, forgiveness, generosity and mercy do you owe, and how will you pay them?

Christmas is the season when you buy this year's gifts with next year's money.

Anonymous

6 December

"We bought the Christmas tree today. We decorated it, and put it in the window and switched on the lights. A magical moment. It was like Christmas had arrived, and the world felt OK again."

Most of us still have a Christmas tree each year; though it might be better to buy a sustainable one and to make sure we dispose of it in an environmentally friendly way. Most of us also have a box of decorations that we keep in the loft and that we unpack with childlike wonder. The decorations themselves usually carry the weight of many memories: things our children made at school as well as decorations passed to us from a previous generation, reminding us of our own childhood.

We usually put a star or an angel at the top of the tree. This even happens in the homes of those who won't be planning any visits to church at Christmas. Yet it gets us back to the heart of the story – the strange announcement to Mary that she would bear God's son; a new star rising, offering the world a different path to follow.

- What stars are you following? What do you really want to get out of life? It doesn't say on anyone's gravestone, they wished they'd spent more time at the office!

- What angels will visit you today? What messages are you listening to? Those siren voices complaining that you aren't good enough, rich enough, clever enough, attractive enough? Or the voices of affirmation that say to you, like they said to Mary, that God thinks you're OK, that he has a purpose for your life, that he can be alive in you. The word angel means 'messenger'. There are messages for you today.

- And why not buy a real ever-new, evergreen Christmas tree in a pot this year, and then you can keep it for next year as well.

- If you have a cut tree, make sure you recycle it. Ninety per cent aren't!

Never worry about the size of your Christmas tree.
In the eyes of children, they are all 30 feet tall.

Larry Wilde

7 December

"I know I should have done this weeks ago, but if I don't tackle that Christmas cake today it will never happen."

Someone told me recently that many new houses are built without a dining room. How very depressing. Is it really the case that many families eat separate pre-cooked meals in separate rooms in front of separate television sets? Cooking together and eating together used to be the glue of community life. Both take time. But both give so much in return.

And for that matter, we don't invite people round for dinner because we think they're hungry. We invite them for their company. It's the human craving for friendship and community that we need to fill.

One of my favourite bits of Christmas is helping make the cake, stirring the ingredients into a bowl, spooning in the brandy. Or preparing the stuffing for the turkey, rolling up my sleeves and scrunching together a bowlful of sausage meat, sage, onion and parsley. It's the only way to get the right consistency. These things need not be lost to us. And once everything's made, invite others to share. If we want to invest in a different sort of Christmas this might be the best place to begin.

- Get out the recipe book. Making a Christmas cake or a Christmas pudding is not that hard and not that expensive. And if you have someone else to do it with, all the better.

- Bring back mealtimes! Start a new regime where dinner is on the table at a certain time and you all sit together.

- And who else will you invite?

- And say grace before you start. Even if you can't give thanks to God, be thankful that there is food on your table when so many in the world today have nothing.

No matter how busy our current lifestyles are, or what is going on outside, family meals are really important . . . I am determined to get families back around the table.

Gordon Ramsay

8   December

"What is the sound of one cracker being pulled? What about all the people who will be on their own at Christmas? What about those who don't have a home, let alone a dining room?"

About half a million people spend Christmas on their own each year. Some do this out of choice, preferring the solitude of their own company to the forced merriment of others. Some do not. Many people are just isolated, alienated, forgotten or abandoned. The overcrowded noisiness of our busy, prosperous culture can be the loneliest place on earth. Some people can go through a whole day with very little human contact. Everything is automated. We interact with our computers and our phones, but not with each other. We know the names of those who live in Albert Square. We've barely spoken to our own next door neighbour.

There's another vast number of people who don't have any home at all. Nobody is sure how many, but last Christmas the charity Crisis served 35,000 meals in its shelters across London. Then there are the half a million or so 'hidden homeless': people living in squats or bedsits, families in temporary accommodation, people sleeping on a friend's sofa.

What is the one thing everyone remembers from the Christmas story? There was no room at the inn. God entered the world through the experience of homelessness and the rejection and isolation that goes with it. How can we reach out to those whose experience is the same today?

- Do you know anyone who might be alone this Christmas?

- What could you do to offer them company?

- Find out about what happens in your local community to support homeless people. As well as national charities like Crisis and Shelter there are often local projects and centres that need support. Offer them some help. Take them some food and warm clothing.

The greatest suffering is being lonely, feeling unloved, having no one. I have come more and more to realize that it is being unwanted that is the worst disease that any human being can ever experience.

Mother Teresa of Calcutta

9   December

"Help! I'm feeling spiritual! I started the shopping today. And coming home, laden with stuff, I heard the Salvation Army playing Christmas carols. I stopped for a moment and listened to them; and for a moment I thought I might even cry. What was that about?"

There is a kind of spiritual something – a longing – inside all human beings. Some of us successfully hide it, ignore it, disguise it or deny it. Some of us delight in its many different manifestations – in art, music, literature or science – without feeling a need to explore it at its source. Others of us are swept away by the first sight of a fresh fall of snow; by the smell of spring in the air, or, at this time of year, by the wide-eyed excitement in the eyes of a child. Philosophers, scientists and psychologists can all offer alternative theories of where this sense of something else comes from, but even so it has not turned Britain into a nation of atheists. Most of us still believe in something. It is as if some sense of God has been hot wired into us.

This doesn't mean there will be a stampede to get to church this Christmas – though interestingly attendances at Christmas are getting bigger year on year. But it does mean that for many people there is an openness to explore who God is, and what life with God is all about.

- Treat yourself to a few minutes of stillness today. See what difference it makes.

- Listen to a piece of music, or read a poem, or just dare to be silent, listening to your own breathing. Peel back the layers of your subterfuge and denial and look again at what your heart longs for and what it believes.

- What are the things that get you back in touch with yourself? Treat yourself to a dose of whatever tickles your fancy; or at least schedule it in for those days after Christmas when you might even have some time – not to kill – but to ravish!

- All the major religions teach about the value of prayer, stillness, solitude and silence. It is possible to build these things into our lives. Find out more about the fine art of doing nothing.

No one in the world can alter truth. All we can do is seek it and live it.

Maximilian Kolbe

10 December

"A few minutes ago my seven-year-old came running into the kitchen, deliriously excited by the fantastic looking toy that had just been paraded before him in the ad break. He told me everything about it; that is, everything except that it costs a fortune and is probably rubbish."

From the plastic toys that they dole out with hamburgers, to the sweets placed enticingly low – and well within toddlers' reach – on the supermarket shelves, to the blanket TV advertising of all sorts of junk food and even junkier toys, advertisers have children in their sights. They know that pester power is here to stay. There might be a child somewhere who is happy with a home-made jumper or a second-hand book, but I've not met them – and they obviously don't watch television! And since it is Father Christmas, not you, who is going to be forking out for all this stuff, what's the problem anyway! They will tick things off in catalogues, write lists of what they want, and send letters to Santa. It is a huge burden on all of us. For the less well off, it must be a nightmare.

There are some diversionary tactics that might help – like hiding the catalogues and controlling the television consumption! – but what's really needed is a proper conversation about what is realistic, what is really worth having, what can be afforded and what those adverts are really doing. This takes time, but of course this is the gift your children need more than anything, the gift of a loving family, and parents who have time.

- Are you planning to give your children everything they want this Christmas except the one thing they need the most – which is you?

- Have you made time to be there for their nativity play, Christingle service or end-of-term show?

- Are you going to sit down with them and talk through what they really want for Christmas?

- Do nothing together. Idle away some time, fold up some paper and make some snowflakes to stick on the window; bake some mince pies together; plan some silly games to play at Christmas. Conversation often flows best when you are happily muddling away together at something like this.

If a child is to keep alive his inborn sense of wonder, he needs the companionship of at least one adult who can share it, rediscovering with him the joy, excitement and mystery of the world we live in.

Rachel Carson

11 December

"Oh no, it's the office party this evening. Another round of boozing, schmoozing and crude canoodling. I don't think I can face it. People are either mind-numbingly polite or back to my place drunk, but very little in-between."

A timely warning from the Royal Society for the Prevention of Accidents: don't sit on the photocopier and copy your bottom; it could lead to serious injury. (Well, that's one less thing to do as Christmas approaches.) But it's not just photocopied buttocks that are causing problems at the annual office party: over-indulgence in the festive season costs British firms over £100 million a year, as people take time off to recover. And along with inhibition alcohol banishes judgement as well. When the dust settles, the headache recedes and the damage is surveyed, relationships as well as businesses can find themselves in the red. Binge drinking is clearly not just a pastime for the young!

There is only one detailed report of Jesus at a party – but what a party! The wine ran out and he famously provided a lot more; and not just any old wine, the very best vintage and in copious quantity. So there's nothing wrong with a drink. In fact, there's nothing wrong with a couple of drinks. But when it is impossible to relax, or interact, or even pluck up the courage to get out of the door, without the Dutch courage of a drink something is terribly wrong. We are rapidly becoming the drunk of Europe. We need to find other ways of enjoying a drink and enjoying life without one.

- Do a quick (and honest!) self assessment: how much do you drink each week? How much do you *depend* on drink to fuel your social life?

- Reconsider the honourable and ancient tradition of the fast. This was what the period leading up to Christmas used to be about: we did without things in order to learn what is truly essential and to appreciate them more when we enjoyed them again.

- The feast is far sweeter when it follows the fast.

They always say time changes things, but you actually have to change them yourself.

Andy Warhol

12 December

"Well, today I did cry. I got out the crib figures and placed them in the makeshift shoebox manger that we have used for years, and remembered how the children used to help me, and just felt life slipping through my fingers."

Some years ago a certain bishop (who had better remain nameless) achieved a little bit of press notoriety when he suggested that the clergy of his diocese fill the aisles of their churches with cow dung and horse manure during the Christmas season. Anything, he said, to get people back to the realities of the story.

There is a gloriously scurrilous and irreverent Spanish tradition of placing an additional figure in the crib. Alongside the Holy Family, angels and shepherds there is also a man squatting in the corner of the stable with his trousers round his ankles. He is *El Caganer*, which means, to put it as politely as I can, 'the great defecator'. Nowadays the figurines are often fashioned after famous people. In Spain last year you could buy President Bush and Pope Benedict XVI! But the tradition itself goes back to the seventeenth century, where a rural culture associated this 'night soil' with fertile fields and successful crops. Today, the tradition lives on mainly to give people something to laugh about – which is no bad thing – but also to bring the story down to earth.

There is a plain and basic reality to this story of birth in a cowshed, of God come down to earth sharing in the waste and wonder of what it is to be human. It is easily obscured. We turn it into something for the children. The Board of Censors would give it at least a 15 rating.

- Why do we put these figures in the crib?
- Who are they?
- What does their story say to us?
- Where do we enter in?
- Dare I stop to look inside?
- Is this a story of God come down to earth? Or just another bit of childhood to be left behind?

Christmas is not as much about opening our presents as opening our hearts.

Janice Maeditere

13 December

"OK, so I've got six people coming to dinner on Christmas Day and I've ordered a 22lb turkey which, if I've estimated it correctly, should be enough to feed forty! I've also ordered a side of bacon and several pounds of sausages. I shall do a supermarket shop next week and stock up with enough stuff to feed the Alamo for several months. And all the shops will open again on Boxing Day – when I'll be hitting the sales."

One of the best bits of Christmas is sitting down to eat. I love the theatre of bringing a turkey (or goose, if I can persuade the family to let me buy one) from the oven to the table. I relish all the preparations – studying the recipe, boiling up the giblets for stock, preparing the stuffing. I carefully work out the intricacies of the timing and post instructions in the kitchen under the heading 'The Turkey Campaign!'

But what is true for presents and shopping and alcohol at Christmas – we massively over-indulge – can also be true for food. What irony! Our chosen method for celebrating God coming to us in such simplicity is days of unrelieved gluttony. But the remedy is also the same: restoring the balance between fasting and feasting. Christmas is worth celebrating, so let the champagne flow and get that turkey in the oven. But it doesn't need to be preceded and followed by weeks of the same. Indeed, the turkey will be all the tastier if the days beforehand have been filled with simpler fare.

- Buy what you need.

- Buy ethically reared poultry. Spend a bit more and eat a bit less.

- Prepare for the feast with the simplicity of the fast.

- And do a bit more of the cooking yourself. There is always one vital ingredient missing in pre-packaged food – the love that only you can stir in.

Christmas has its critics and, if we were honest, I'm sure each one of us has, at some time, wished we could quietly quit the planet and come back when it is over. On the other hand, at what other time of the year can we turn our minds to the sheer joy of feasting? The sharing of fine food and wines with family and friends is a deeply ingrained human (as well as religious) activity, without which our lives would surely be diminished.

Delia Smith

14 December

"Bedecked in the traditional tea-towel – *de rigueur* for any first-century Palestinian sheep farmer – my youngest son was shepherd number 27 in the school nativity play today. Surrounded by a sea of video cameras (why do people want to experience everything second-hand through their TV and effectively miss the live performance?), I wept again."

School nativity plays tell the basic story in a way that is often overly sentimental – stables become the most lovely place to give birth, and shepherds quite the most welcome guests – but they also relate the events with an uncluttered impact: ordinary men and women caught up in astonishing events and working out how to respond.

An angel asks Mary if she will be the mother of God's son. She pauses for a moment, ponders the fearful and unpredictable possibilities of this request, and says yes. Joseph could divorce her, but unlike most middle-aged men he is still able to listen to his dreams and supports her instead.

One by one doors are closed in this family's face, a first example of all the other doors that will close for Jesus in the future. But among the very poor and those who know their need of God – what the Bible calls the poor in spirit – Jesus finds a home. He is born in a stable. He is visited by shepherds.

The nativity play also offers another challenge: to see through the costumes, the words and the sea of cameras to the children acting out the parts. God always favours the little ones. The ones on the edge are always the heroes in the Bible. Funnily enough, the Christmas story enacted by children is the Christmas story closest to its truth. God is among us; working through us.

- Receive the Christmas story as a child.

- Take some child-like delight in what is happening around you today.

- Be amazed at the breath in your lungs, the pulse in your wrist, the wind in the trees, the sun upon your face, the water in your tap, the stars in the sky and the smiles on the faces of all the people who will look at you as if you are mad when you kneel down in the street and give thanks for the profligate goodness of the world that is given to us today.

- Remember that you learned life's really important lessons at nursery school; sit still, share your toys and clean up after yourself. If we managed these three there would be peace in the world!

The most beautiful thing we can experience is the mysterious. It is the source of all true art and all science. He to whom this emotion is a stranger, who can no longer pause to wonder and stand rapt in awe, is as good as dead: his eyes are closed.

Albert Einstein

15 December

"There are so many Christmas lights on the house round the corner that it must be burning its very own hole in the ozone layer. It is over-the-top fantastic and hugely depressing all at once. Am I the only one who is confused?"

Although many Christmas lights are becoming more energy efficient, it is still estimated that you would have to plant a great forest of trees to compensate for the carbon emissions generated by the miles of lights that illuminate our city centres and, increasingly, our homes. In many streets neighbours vie with one another for the most extravagant and outlandish displays.

It is magical. But it is also a sad reflection on how little we have grasped of the environmental challenge that is facing us. We need changes in technology, but more than anything we need a change of heart; a desire and a determination to do things more simply, to consume less and to change ingrained habits. There is little sign that this is happening. The glare of the Christmas lights just tell me that we all think this is someone else's problem. Well, it will be – our children's – unless we change. They will inherit the chaos and misery we are sleep-walking into.

Can we see through the dazzle of these twinkling lights to the one star that shone over Bethlehem and which offers the world a new direction? This was the challenge to those wise men of old: that the wisdom that had served them well must now be re-examined and reconfigured in the light of some very startling new information.

- Switch off the lights, or at least ration how long they are on for.

- Buy those LED lights, and fill your house with those instead.

- Christmas present problem solved: buy everyone energy efficient light bulbs and rechargeable batteries – and get some for yourself while you're at it!

- Work out your carbon footprint – and resolve to reduce it. There are lots of resources on the Web for working out your carbon footprint and offsetting your carbon emissions, such as the UK Carbon Footprint project at www.carbonfootprint.com, or the Big Green Switch at www.biggreenswitch.co.uk.

- See the Church of England's Shrinking your Carbon Footprint campaign at www.cofe.anglican.org.

- Switch to a green energy supplier. Again, there are details on the Web and help in switching at websites like the Green Helpline at www.greenhelpline.com.

Unless we change the direction we are heading, we might end up where we are going.

Chinese proverb

16 December

"The moral issue of our day: to buy a *Big Issue*, or not to buy a *Big Issue*. Now that *is* the question."

I remember someone saying they would like to discuss their spiritual life with me. 'That's fine', I replied. 'Please make sure you bring your credit card statement with you.' They were slightly taken aback. 'It was my spiritual life I was hoping to discuss', they began. 'Well', I explained, 'whether we like it or not, what we do with our money is the clearest possible indicator of what we think our spiritual life is actually about.'

Spirituality is not some vague, mushy feeling of goodwill towards the universe; it is the way our experience of God is sustained and expressed. If we believe God has a concern for all the universe, then so should we. If we believe God is concerned about those who have little at Christmas, then so should we. Christmas is a time of crippling difficulty for many people who live below the poverty line and inhabit the shadows of our increasingly flash and affluent society. Somewhere – probably somewhere very close – there is someone worse off than you. There is no room at the inn because we've booked all the rooms. How can we re-order priorities to make space for others?

- Get out your credit card statement and your bank statement and see where your money actually goes.

- Is there a standing order for a charity? Or is charitable giving a matter of seeing what's left over?

- Make sure you give at least one gift to the poor this Christmas.

Generosity isn't measured by how much you give; but by how much is left over when you've finished giving.

Richard Inwood

17 December

"Oh no, another moral dilemma. Do I watch *Coronation Street* or *EastEnders* on Christmas Day? Or flick between the two? Or watch one and then watch the other on i-Player? And with all the plots simmering towards a boiling point explosion of misery and grief, revenge and disappointment . . . I can hardly wait."

It used to be the Queen's speech that united us as a nation. Now it is more likely to be a brutal stabbing in the Queen Vic. Even though most of us now consume mass media in very different ways – whilst one member of the family is watching one thing on one television, someone else is watching something else in another room, and another person is downloading clips from YouTube and someone else is playing on their phone or X-Box – the soaps have almost managed to pull us all together around a climactic family breakdown, tempestuous affair, or tragic death: and the climax always comes around teatime on Christmas Day.

We live in networks: either virtual communities like MySpace or Facebook, or television communities like *Emmerdale* and *EastEnders*. Sometimes they seem more real than the actual communities we inhabit. And along with sport, another way we get our sense of belonging today, they provide the common experiences that we talk about most.

But we don't necessarily know much about each other. Indeed, the local church is one of the few places left where people of all shapes and sizes, ages and races (Spurs and Arsenal fans meeting in harmony!) gather together regularly. Shepherds and kings were invited to the stables at Bethlehem. Regardless of rank, race, class or caste you are invited today.

- Do I know my next door neighbour's name?
- Do I only ever mix with people like myself?
- Is there anywhere I go where there are people of other races or religions?
- Make a pledge to start a conversation with someone you hardly know.

The lion and the calf shall lie down together, but the calf won't get much sleep.

Woody Allen

18 December

"One week to go. All the family are coming to stay. They will arrive on Christmas morning. And they won't be leaving until the day after Boxing Day. That means we will all be together for at least 48 hours. Now where did I put those tranquilizers?"

The American comedian George Burns defined happiness as 'having a large, loving, close knit family in another city'. But, oh dear, Christmas is the time of year when you all get together. Surviving Christmas inevitably means surviving relatives. Perhaps it is wise to remember that just as you didn't choose them to be your family, they didn't choose you either. There is only one remedy: you are just going to have to forego that opportunity to score points and settle accounts and love them instead. The worms are going to have to stay in the can.

Jesus doesn't ask us to love everyone; he asks us to love our neighbour. Loving everyone is relatively easy. Most of us can muster a general feeling of goodwill towards an unspecific someone, so long as you never actually have to live with them. But to love your neighbour, to love your family, to love those very particular and hugely irritating people that are actually with you now, well this is much more difficult. But it is the only hope for peace in our world.

- Instead of looking with delight at the splinter in your brother's eye, remove the log from your own.

- OK, so you don't always like your family, but that doesn't excuse you from loving them, and offering them the generosity and kindness that you long to receive.

- In fact, when it comes to generosity and kindness, you will reap what you sow.

- Plan some things to do together that are not just watching TV. In my family we always play games. It is a great leveller. Arrange a Boxing Day walk. Book some tickets for the local panto.

- God's love for the world is communicated through a person who, like us, was born in a family. God knows what they're like. He knows they're not always easy.

Family is just accident . . . They don't mean to get on your nerves. They don't even mean to be your family, they just are.

Marsha Norman

19 December

"Yes, but my family is weirder than most."

As a child I was told that Father Christmas had a hole in his sack where Smarties leaked out wherever he went. So every Christmas began by following the Smartie trail around the house to see where presents might be hidden. Of course, I thought this happened in everybody's house so it was a bit of a rude awakening when at school I discovered this was not the case. Not only did it cause me to question Father Christmas himself, it was a first experience of just how embarrassing one's family can be, even when they're intending to be nice!

This is the real truth. To one degree or other, we all find our families embarrassing. It's something we all have in common. And the other sobering fact that we seem hell-bent on avoiding is that we are all members of our family. What really irritates us about them is that they are so like us! And here's another uncomfortable truth: we are part of a common humanity. We all have the same frailties, insecurities, anxieties and heartfelt longings. We are all a bit weird. We are all flawed. We are all less than the people we want to be. We all get embarrassed by ourselves and by those around us. We all cause embarrassment to others.

Christmas can be a time when we let this get on top of us. Wouldn't it be better to take the medicine on offer? To accept these frailties, and then to do two other things: first, accept yourself as the flawed and beautiful person that you are; and second, have a very good laugh at your own foolishness and enjoy the foolishness of others, especially those you're going to be spending the next week with. After all, this is supposed to be the season of goodwill.

- Take yourself less seriously.
- The best comedies will not be on television this Christmas. They will be around your own table, if you can but see them.
- Re-imagine the peoples of the world as a hugely complex, extremely muddled, wonderfully odd and riotously funny family. Enjoy the differences. Take proper account of the deep-seated similarities.
- Say sorry a bit more.
- Say thank you.

One of the symptoms of an approaching nervous breakdown is the belief that one's work is terribly important.

Bertrand Russell

20 December

"So here's the big one. What do I tell the children about Father Christmas? And when?"

I think we rather let down our eldest child. We never told him the Christmas story. At least not properly. We told him all that stuff about Jesus, but the other Christmas story, the one about Santa and sleigh bells and red-nosed reindeer and chimneys, well, somehow that one passed us by. We were not complete puritans on the subject. He did leave a stocking at the end of his bed and we did tell him that Father Christmas left presents, and of course he picked up a lot from school and television, who are very diligent in making sure everyone is up to scratch in these matters, but we didn't go into detail. So much so that when I realized he was a bit shaky on the subject I went out and bought a copy of *Spot the Dog's First Christmas* so that he could be suitably instructed!

But it needn't be one story or the other: even the replete, white-bearded, unstintingly jolly twenty-first century Father Christmas has his origin in St Nicholas, who cared for the poor and distributed gifts. It is a Christian story. However, many people leave Jesus behind with Father Christmas. He's good for children – baby Jesus definitely has the 'Ah' factor – but not for grown-ups. And yet Jesus persists. He grows up. That child in the manger becomes a man whose teaching and example challenge and change the world. And whilst I don't know any adults who still believe in Father Christmas, many continue to follow Jesus. Indeed, many who didn't believe in him as a child start following him as adults.

So enjoy the Father Christmas story with your children, and when they question it help them to leave it behind. But enjoy the story of Jesus as well. And when they question it, allow it to lead them forward. It can show them how to inhabit the world.

- Read the story to your children. There are good children's Bibles easily available.

- Read the story yourself – but make sure you get a modern translation.

- Enjoy the Father Christmas story, and invent a few weird family traditions of your own. Make a Smartie trail for your kids this Christmas leading from the foot of their bed to the presents under the tree, or a hidden present somewhere in the house.

- If you don't have one already, invest in a crib and give it pride of place in the house, and light a candle by it in the evening.

Your children need your presence more than your presents.

Jesse Jackson

21 December

"And what do I tell them about God? And how, when I don't know what I think myself?"

It's easy to get believing in God all round the wrong way. We think we need to understand and have all the answers – or at least most of them – before we can believe. Many people find it works the other way round: they believe in order to understand. They start from the premise that it might be true, that those feelings inside them telling them that there's more to life than what they see around them might be right after all, and then, inch by inch, as they participate in the life of the church and try to behave in a way that matches up to these beliefs, understanding slowly grows.

This is called faith. It's not the same as certainty. It always includes doubts. And there's never a time when all the questions are answered. One question leads to another. And if your children ask you questions then give them honest answers. Don't pretend you know it all. But don't pretend you don't know it all either. Most of us have a bit of faith, it just needs nurturing. Find a place for both you and your children where questions can be explored.

One of the names Jesus is given at his birth is Emmanuel. It means 'God with us'. The Christmas story is about God revealed in a person, living among us, and known through relationship. Just like all human relationships, this one with God requires honesty and trust. What we need to do now is give it a go.

- Will you go to church this Christmas and test out this hypothesis of love?

- What for you are the biggest obstacles that get in the way of believing?

- How might you be able to remove them? Who could help you?

- What could you and your family do to find out more about the Christian faith?

In Jesus the whole test passing, brownie point earning rigmarole of the human race has been cancelled for lack of interest on God's part. All he needs from us is a simple Yes or No, and off to work he goes.

Robert Farrar Capon

22 December

"So I went to a carol service. It was OK. Not great. Not awful. At least I knew the songs. But it was also disturbing. Something coming at me under the radar. A music that was unfamiliar, and yet the most pleasing and welcome sound I have ever heard: the voice of home."

The human heart is made for community with God. All the joyful, creative things that thrill the human heart – music and dance and football and poetry, walking in the Pennines, or cross stitching a tapestry – are echoes of the joyful, creative God whose overflowing love created it all in the first place and who made us creative. Whenever our heart misses a beat, either in joy or sorrow, we are in touch with the God who is always on the lookout for his beloved – that is us.

The Christmas story is the story of God's searching for us: and at last he speaks to us in a language we can understand, the language of another human life. You might not have been looking for God. You might have assumed God was an idea whose time has been and gone. You might have decided Richard Dawkins is right. But then something happens and your present understanding of the world just seems too small, and you are transported, if only for a moment, into a different world where all the joys you've ever known are gathered together into one almighty now. This might be wishful thinking. It might be an attack of wind. It might be one too many vodka and tonics. But there are still millions of people who find in this story something no other story can offer.

Christmas carols tell the story. They may not always do it very well, and sometimes there is too generous a dose of sentimental twaddle. But they move us. They speak to the heart. They reanimate hope.

- What things bring you the greatest joy?
- What moments in your life are so inexplicably wonderful that you cannot comprehend them without using the language of the soul, the heart, the spirit?
- OK, so your heart is just a big muscle pumping your very necessary blood around your very mortal body; but it is also something else, something that cannot be defined or understood without another sort of language, that seems like an echo from another life.
- Get out the mistletoe: who do you want to kiss?

The best remedy for those who are afraid, lonely or unhappy is to go outside, somewhere where they can be quiet, alone with the heavens, nature and God. Because only then does one feel that all is as it should be and that God wishes to see people happy, amidst the simple beauty of nature.

Anne Frank

23 December

"Apart from stuffing the turkey, icing the cake, baking mince pies, wrapping the presents, buying the presents for the people I haven't yet got round to, making a wreath to put on the front door (because we always put a wreath on the front door and everyone is nagging me to do it), replacing the fused lights on the tree, going to the supermarket for the shopping, making yet more mince pies, going back to the supermarket for the things I have forgotten, then I'm completely ready for Christmas. There's just one question: will my Christmas be good enough?"

One of the best Christmas dinners I ever had was when I was staying at my brother's, and the very expensive free-range, organic turkey that he had ordered got lost in the post. He kept phoning up the company, and they kept assuring him it would be there by Christmas. But it never arrived. So we tucked into whatever was available – some chicken thighs out of the freezer, sausages, stuffing, sprouts, and thoroughly enjoyed a scrumptious feast.

So let me tell you a story. There once was a king who was completely overburdened by work, stress and all the pressures of running a busy and successful kingdom. At his wits' end, he sought the advice of a holy sage: 'What must I do to be happy?' he asked. 'There is but one cure for the king,' the sage replied, 'you must spend one night in the shirt of a happy man.'

Messengers were dispatched throughout the kingdom to search for a man who was truly happy. But everyone they found was also weighed down with misery and overburdened with stress. But at last they found a man – a poor beggar – who sat smiling by the side of the road. They asked him if he was truly happy and had no sorrows. He replied that he was. So they explained that the king must sleep one night in the shirt of a truly happy man, and that he would pay a large sum of money to procure such a shirt. The poor man burst into uncontrollable laughter: 'I'm sorry,' he replied, 'I cannot oblige the king. I do not own a shirt.'

- It's not what you have, or what you don't have, but what you do with it that counts.

- So forget about what you don't have; let go of the things you no longer have time to fit in. Enjoy what you do have instead, and make the most of the time you have now – after all it is the only time you possess with any certainty.

- And why not start manifesting a few other crazy signs of happiness and goodwill. Say hello to the people you pass in the street, smile a bit more, and laugh at your adversities. I once read a survey comparing the number of times a child smiles each day to the number of times an adult does. The difference was alarming. Children's smiles outnumbered adults by about ten to one. Let's bump up our average!

People can't concentrate properly on blowing other people to pieces if their minds are poisoned by thoughts suitable to the twenty-fifth of December.

Ogden Nash

24 December

"I'm not dreaming of a white Christmas, I'm dreaming of a connected Christmas, a rainbow Christmas, where I can see and enjoy all the different colours, and where somewhere in the middle of it I can stop for a moment and take it all in."

One of my best Christmas memories is from the church in Chichester where I was the parish priest. Because the building was so small, and because every other available inch of space was needed for chairs, we used to put the crib underneath the altar.

One Christmas morning, about halfway through the service, a little girl, Miriam, toddled up to the front of the church. She can only have been about two or three at the time. For several minutes she stood before the crib, gazing intently at the figures. Then, very carefully, so as not to wake the baby, she stepped inside and sat down. And as people looked at the crib that Christmas, as well as the shepherds and the angels and the ox and the ass, and Mary and Joseph and the baby Jesus, they saw Miriam. She sat there for the rest of the service, content to have become part of the story. She was the best Christmas sermon I have ever experienced. I think this is also the best example I can muster of the how to get ready for Christmas this year.

- Now that all the preparations are done – or at least now that there is no more time for any more preparing – stop, and find a place of quiet.

- Be still. Get inside the story. Sit down. Make yourself smaller. In your imagination go to Bethlehem. Bend beneath the lintel of the door of the stable and come in.

- God comes to us in the vulnerability of a child. We can come to him in stillness. We can find him in silence. And Christmas can be put back together. And enjoyed.

Christmas renews our youth by stirring our wonder. The capacity for wonder has been called our most pregnant human faculty, for in it are born our art, our science, our religion.

Ralph Sockman

25 December

"So here it is Merry Christmas, everybody's having fun; look to the future now it's only just begun."

So sang Slade all those years ago (and in every shop in England for the past six weeks!), but here's the nub, the real clue to the future: Mary listened to angels and found things born in her; travelled great distances and found things given to her; Joseph listened to dreams and found reality; the shepherds left their work and found their joy; and wise men abandoned the wisdom, charts, maps, compasses and guidebooks that they already possessed to follow a new star that was rising before them.

In order to listen and in order to dream; in order to smile with joy and in order to travel vast distances; in order to learn new ways and trust new leaders; you first need to stop, to take stock of what you really want from life and where you will really find the direction, affirmation and purposes you seek.

It is the longest journey you will ever make. It requires a complete reorientation. It is also the shortest – its beginning and end can be found in the stable at Bethlehem, a way in a manger. So, may I wish you a defragged and rebooted Christmas this year – things back in the right order, first things first, and with it the joy and peace that is the heart of the Christmas story.

- Build one or two little extras into Christmas Day this year.

- Maybe say a prayer before you eat, or at least have a moment of collective silence as you give thanks for all you have received.

- Find that place of quiet that you are looking for and reflect on all that you have been trying to put back together as you have read this book, and make some early New Year resolutions.

- Raise you glass and drink a toast to the God of Christmas who visits you today.

One of the most glorious messes in the world is the mess created in the living room on Christmas Day. Don't clean it up too quickly.

Andy Rooney

A few next steps

- Find out about the Christian faith at the *ReJesus* web site – www.rejesus.co.uk
- Find out about your local church at *A Church Near You* web site – www.achurchnearyou.com
- Find out about prayer and stillness. If you've found this book helpful you might like:

    – *Do Nothing to Change Your Life* by Stephen Cottrell

    – *Praying through Life* by Stephen Cottrell.

They're both published by Church House Publishing and available online from their web site at www.chpublishing.co.uk.

Sources

The number of the page on which each quotation appears is printed in brackets after the published source.

Robert Farrar Capon, *The Mystery of Christ and Why We Don't Get It*, Eerdmans, 1993 (p. 51).

Rachel Carson, *The Sense of Wonder* (1952), Harper & Row, 1965 (p. 29).

Anne Frank, *The Diary of a Young Girl* (1952), definitive edition, Doubleday, 1995 (p. 53).

Garrison Keillor, *Leaving Home*, Viking/Penguin, 1987 (p. 6).

Andrew Marr, 'What Christmas presence?', *The Observer*, 19 December 1999 (p. 6).

Marsha Norman, *Night Mother*, Hill & Wang, 1983 (p. 45).

Gordon Ramsay, *Gordon Ramsey's Sunday Lunch and Other Recipes from the F Word*, Quadrille Publishing Ltd, 2006 (p. 23).

Delia Smith, *Delia Smith's Christmas*, BBC Books, 1999 (p. 35).

Andy Warhol, *The Philosophy of Andy Warhol*, Harcourt, 1975 (p. 31).